The FOLENS Ordnance Survey

UK ATLAS

PATRICIA HARRISON

STEVE HARRISON

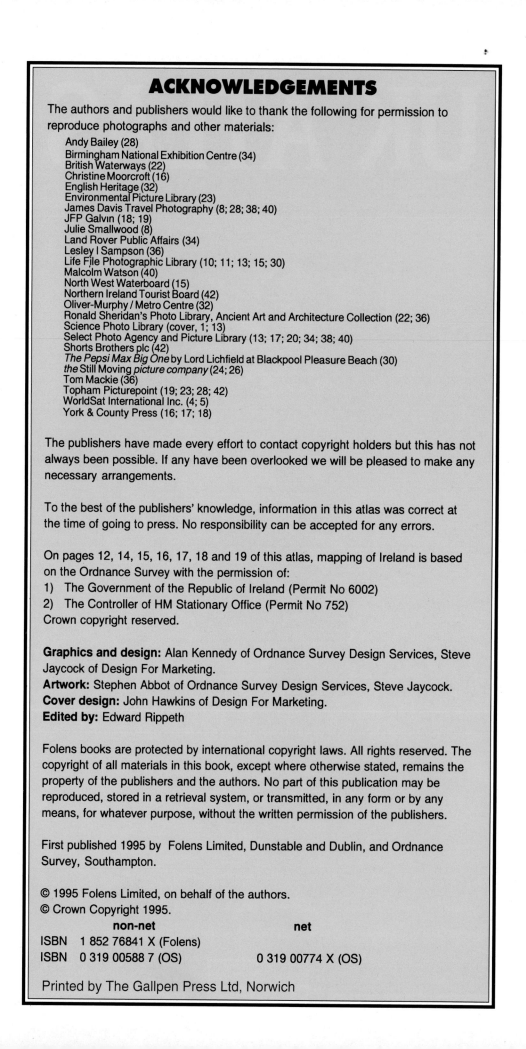

ACKNOWLEDGEMENTS

The authors and publishers would like to thank the following for permission to reproduce photographs and other materials:

Andy Bailey (28)
Birmingham National Exhibition Centre (34)
British Waterways (22)
Christine Moorcroft (16)
English Heritage (32)
Environmental Picture Library (23)
James Davis Travel Photography (8; 28; 38; 40)
JFP Galvin (18; 19)
Julie Smallwood (8)
Land Rover Public Affairs (34)
Lesley I Sampson (36)
Life File Photographic Library (10; 11; 13; 15; 30)
Malcolm Watson (40)
North West Waterboard (15)
Northern Ireland Tourist Board (42)
Oliver-Murphy / Metro Centre (32)
Ronald Sheridan's Photo Library, Ancient Art and Architecture Collection (22; 36)
Science Photo Library (cover, 1; 13)
Select Photo Agency and Picture Library (13; 17; 20; 34; 38; 40)
Shorts Brothers plc (42)
The Pepsi Max Big One by Lord Lichfield at Blackpool Pleasure Beach (30)
the Still Moving *picture company* (24; 26)
Tom Mackie (36)
Topham Picturepoint (19; 23; 28; 42)
WorldSat International Inc. (4; 5)
York & County Press (16; 17; 18)

The publishers have made every effort to contact copyright holders but this has not always been possible. If any have been overlooked we will be pleased to make any necessary arrangements.

To the best of the publishers' knowledge, information in this atlas was correct at the time of going to press. No responsibility can be accepted for any errors.

On pages 12, 14, 15, 16, 17, 18 and 19 of this atlas, mapping of Ireland is based on the Ordnance Survey with the permission of:
1) The Government of the Republic of Ireland (Permit No 6002)
2) The Controller of HM Stationary Office (Permit No 752)
Crown copyright reserved.

Graphics and design: Alan Kennedy of Ordnance Survey Design Services, Steve Jaycock of Design For Marketing.
Artwork: Stephen Abbot of Ordnance Survey Design Services, Steve Jaycock.
Cover design: John Hawkins of Design For Marketing.
Edited by: Edward Rippeth

First published 1995 by Folens Limited, Dunstable and Dublin, and Ordnance Survey, Southampton.

© 1995 Folens Limited, on behalf of the authors.
© Crown Copyright 1995.

	non-net	net
ISBN	1 852 76841 X (Folens)	
ISBN	0 319 00588 7 (OS)	0 319 00774 X (OS)

Printed by The Gallpen Press Ltd, Norwich

FOLENS
Ordnance Survey

UK ATLAS

PAT HARRISON   STEVE HARRISON

CONTENTS

EUROPE from Space

Weather satellites circle the earth at a height of about 820km and send back hundreds of images. These are pieced together to form a large image without clouds. Shading is added to make the height of the land clearer.

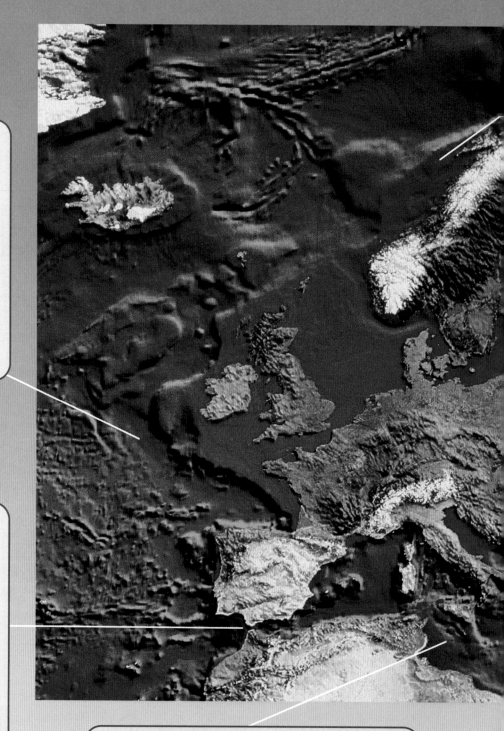

The Atlantic Ocean lies between Europe and America. It is probably named after Atlantis, a large island from Greek legend, which was believed to have been destroyed by an earthquake. At its deepest point the Atlantic is 8648m deep. This is almost as deep as Mount Everest is high!

The Strait of Gibraltar is only 13km across. It separates Africa and Europe, and the Mediterranean Sea from the Atlantic Ocean. In ancient legend the two large rocks north and south of the strait were once joined. Hercules was said to have parted them. That is why they were once known as the pillars of Hercules. Today we call them the Rock of Gibraltar and Jebel Musa.

The Mediterranean Sea is between Europe to the north and Africa to the south and Asia to the east. Mediterranean means centre of the Earth! In the past, Europeans knew nothing of America or Australia. They thought all the world's land surrounded the Mediterranean.

The seas in the far north freeze over in winter. The Norwegian Sea and the Barents Sea are both part of the Arctic Ocean.

Lake Ladoga is Europe's largest lake. It is joined to the Gulf of Finland by the River Neva.

The Ural Mountains mark the Eastern edge of Europe. Beyond them lies Asia. They stretch from the Arctic Circle in the north to the Caspian Sea.

The Volga is Europe's largest river. It is 3685km long.

The Caspian Sea is the largest inland sea in the world. Its western shore is in Europe. It has no tide. Its deepest point is about 1000m deep.

The Caucasus Mountains stand between Europe and Asia. They stretch west–east between the Black Sea and the Caspian Sea. The highest peak is Mount Elbrus which is 5633m high.

The Bosporus is the stretch of water which links the Mediterranean Sea and the Black Sea. It also separates Europe and Asia. The Bosporus is 27km long and is only 600m across at its narrowest point.

EUROPE Political

Population

The total population of Europe is almost 700 million. One in seven of the world's population lives in Europe.

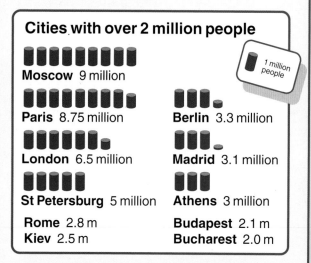

Cities with over 2 million people

1 million people

Moscow 9 million

Paris 8.75 million   Berlin 3.3 million

London 6.5 million   Madrid 3.1 million

St Petersburg 5 million   Athens 3 million

Rome 2.8 m   Budapest 2.1 m
Kiev 2.5 m   Bucharest 2.0 m

Living in Town and Country

The population of a country can be divided into those who live in towns (urban population) and those who live in the countryside (rural population). The percentage of people in rural areas is falling steadily.

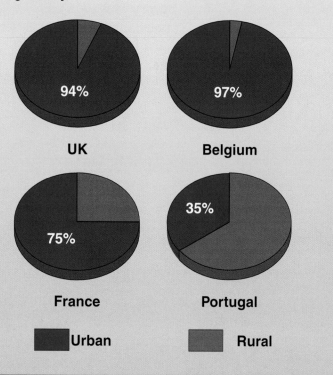

94% UK

97% Belgium

75% France

35% Portugal

■ Urban   ■ Rural

Population density is the number of people living in a square area of land 1km long and 1km wide (a square kilometre). To work out the population density of a country we divide the population by area of land in square kilometres.

$$\frac{\text{Population}}{\text{Area of land}} = \text{Population density}$$

The population density for the whole of Europe is 96 people per sq km. Only Asia has a higher density.

Netherlands 366   Iceland 2

People per sq km

Netherlands	366	Spain	78
Belgium	323	Ireland	53
UK	234	Sweden	19
Germany	218	Finland	15
Italy	189	Norway	13
France	102	Iceland	2

Travel

In the past, travel to the capitals of Europe was often slow, uncomfortable and expensive. Today more and more people visit capital cities for weekend breaks or business. London's airports have the best international connections in the world. The new Channel Tunnel provides a direct rail link to European capitals.

Distances from London

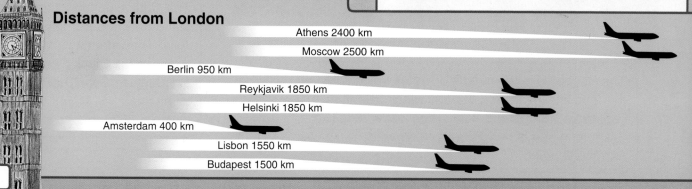

Athens 2400 km

Moscow 2500 km

Berlin 950 km

Reykjavik 1850 km

Helsinki 1850 km

Amsterdam 400 km

Lisbon 1550 km

Budapest 1500 km

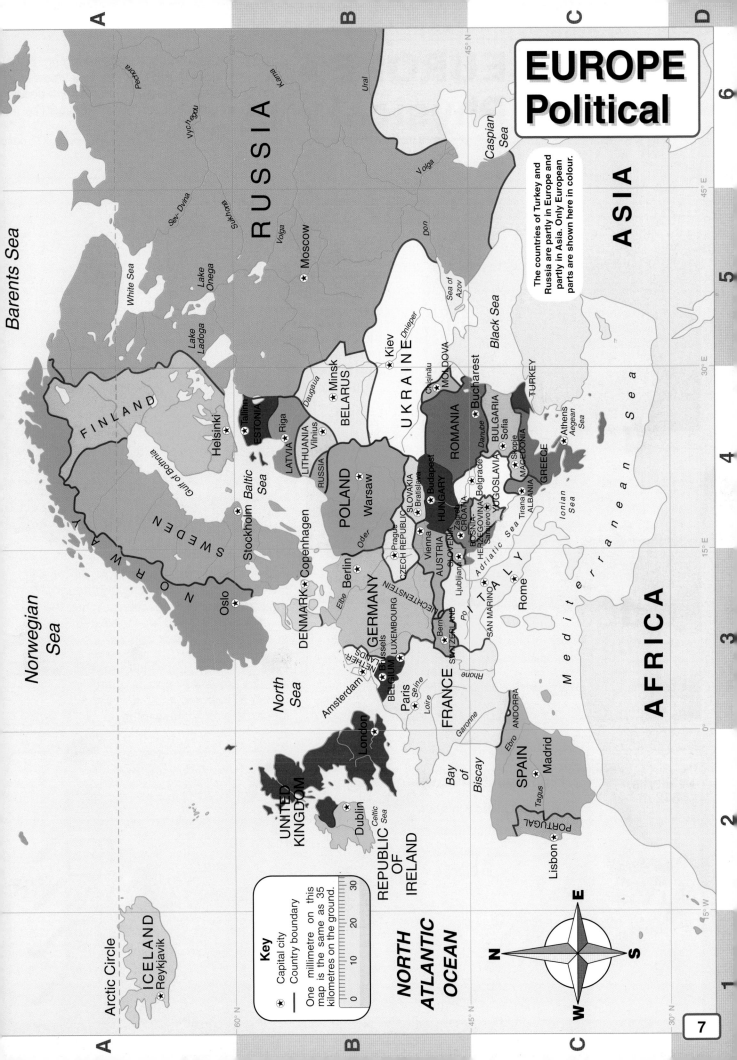

EUROPE
Political

The countries of Turkey and Russia are partly in Europe and partly in Asia. Only European parts are shown here in colour.

Key
- ★ Capital city
- — Country boundary

One millimetre on this map is the same as 35 kilometres on the ground.

0 10 20 30

Seas and Oceans: Barents Sea, Norwegian Sea, North Sea, Celtic Sea, NORTH ATLANTIC OCEAN, White Sea, Baltic Sea, Gulf of Bothnia, Bay of Biscay, Mediterranean Sea, Adriatic Sea, Ionian Sea, Aegean Sea, Black Sea, Sea of Azov, Caspian Sea

Countries and Capitals:
- ICELAND — Reykjavik
- NORWAY — Oslo
- SWEDEN — Stockholm
- FINLAND — Helsinki
- RUSSIA — Moscow
- ESTONIA — Tallinn
- LATVIA — Riga
- LITHUANIA — Vilnius
- BELARUS — Minsk
- UKRAINE — Kiev
- POLAND — Warsaw
- DENMARK — Copenhagen
- UNITED KINGDOM — London
- REPUBLIC OF IRELAND — Dublin
- NETHERLANDS — Amsterdam
- BELGIUM — Brussels
- LUXEMBOURG
- GERMANY — Berlin
- FRANCE — Paris
- SPAIN — Madrid
- PORTUGAL — Lisbon
- ANDORRA
- SWITZERLAND — Bern
- LIECHTENSTEIN
- CZECH REPUBLIC — Prague
- AUSTRIA — Vienna
- SLOVAKIA — Bratislava
- HUNGARY — Budapest
- SLOVENIA — Ljubljana
- CROATIA — Zagreb
- BOSNIA-HERZEGOVINA — Sarajevo
- YUGOSLAVIA — Belgrade
- ITALY — Rome
- SAN MARINO
- ALBANIA — Tirana
- MACEDONIA — Skopje
- BULGARIA — Sofia
- ROMANIA — Bucharest
- MOLDOVA — Chişinău
- GREECE — Athens
- TURKEY
- ASIA
- AFRICA

Rivers and Lakes: Pechora, Vychegda, Sev. Dvina, Sukhona, Kama, Ural, Volga, Don, Dnieper, Daugava, Lake Ladoga, Lake Onega, Oder, Elbe, Seine, Loire, Garonne, Ebro, Tagus, Rhône, Po, Danube

Arctic Circle

45° N, 60° N, 30° N, 45° N
15° W, 0°, 15° E, 30° E, 45° E

7

EUROPE Physical

The physical world is always changing, but it is a very slow change. At different times in the distant past, parts of Europe have been covered by deserts, by warm seas and by ice. Europe is still changing.

New land can appear. In the last few years, volcanic activity around Iceland has created new islands. The steam from this geyser is evidence of the active heat beneath the surface.

The fjords of Norway were formed by ice sheets (glaciers) which carved through the rock forming deep valleys. When the climate warmed and the ice melted the sea flowed into these valleys.

Glaciers are still active in Europe today. As they move they scrape great boulders from mountain sides and loosen the rock below them.

High mountains and long rivers

The United Kingdom's rivers and mountains are small compared to many in Europe.

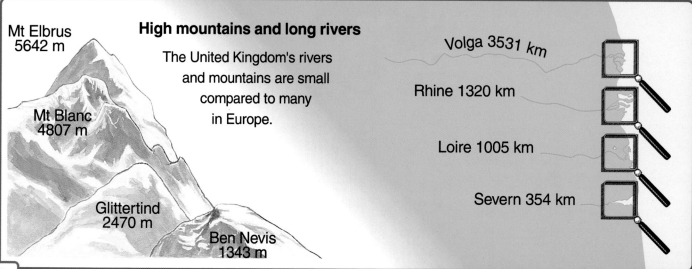

Mt Elbrus 5642 m

Mt Blanc 4807 m

Glittertind 2470 m

Ben Nevis 1343 m

Volga 3531 km

Rhine 1320 km

Loire 1005 km

Severn 354 km

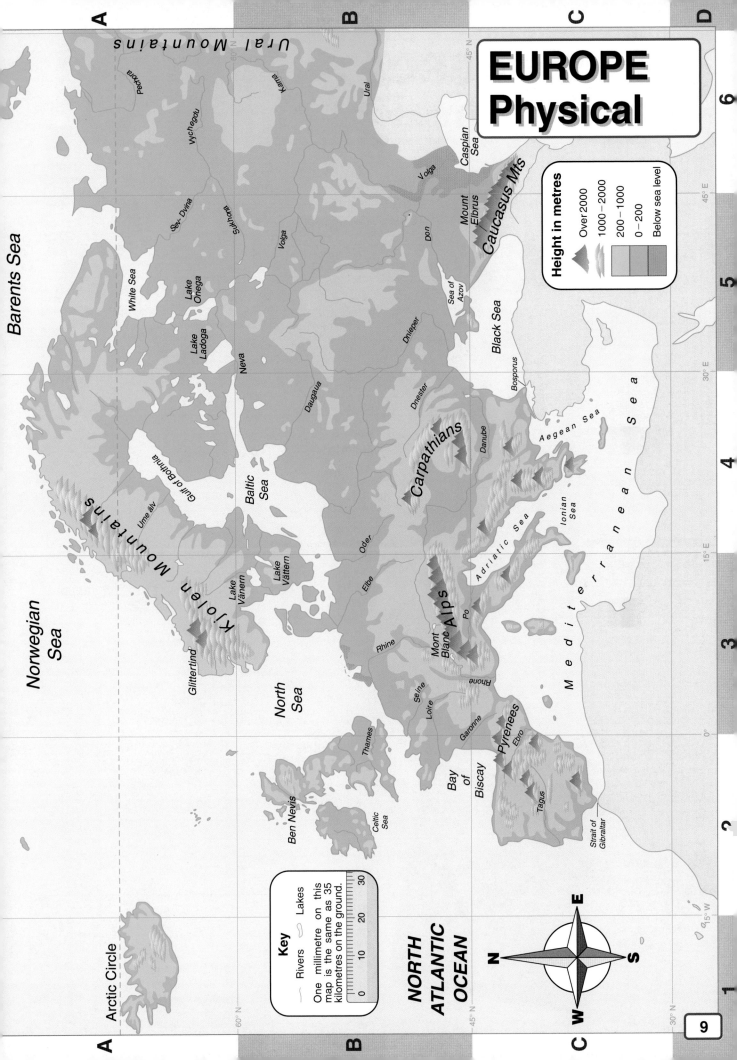

EUROPE
Physical

Height in metres

▲	Over 2000
	1000 – 2000
	200 – 1000
	0 – 200
	Below sea level

Key

— Rivers
⬭ Lakes

One millimetre on this map is the same as 35 kilometres on the ground.

0   10   20   30

Labels on map:

Ural Mountains
Pechora
Kama
Ural
Vychegda
Sev- Dvina
Sukhona
Volga
Volga
Don
Sea of Azov
Caspian Sea
Mount Elbrus
Caucasus Mts
Barents Sea
White Sea
Lake Onega
Lake Ladoga
Neva
Daugaua
Dnieper
Dnester
Black Sea
Bosporus
Aegean Sea
Norwegian Sea
Gulf of Bothnia
Ume älv
Kjolen Mountains
Glittertind
Lake Vänern
Lake Vättern
Baltic Sea
Oder
Elbe
Rhine
Carpathians
Danube
Po
Adriatic Sea
Ionian Sea
Mediterranean Sea
Alps
Mont Blanc
Rhone
Seine
Loire
Garonne
Thames
North Sea
Ben Nevis
Celtic Sea
Bay of Biscay
Ebro
Pyrenees
Tagus
Strait of Gibraltar
Arctic Circle

NORTH ATLANTIC OCEAN

60° N
45° N
30° N
15° W
0°
15° E
30° E
45° E

N   E   S   W

9

EUROPE in winter

ASIA

ASIA

AFRICA

The Alps. High mountains and bright sunshine mean good skiing conditions.

Northern Finland. In northern Europe the winter sun shines for only a few hours each day.

Athens

Temperature Range 20°C

Rainfall Total 402 mm

J F M A M J J A S O N D

°C: 40 30 20 10 0 -10 -20
mm: 250 200 150 100 50 0

Moscow

Temperature Range 32°C

Rainfall Total 624 mm

J F M A M J J A S O N D

°C: 40 30 20 10 0 -10 -20
mm: 250 200 150 100 50 0

London

Temperature Range 16°C

Rainfall Total 593 mm

J F M A M J J A S O N D

°C: 40 30 20 10 0 -10 -20
mm: 250 200 150 100 50 0

Average rainfall and temperatures in Europe

Barents Sea

White Sea

• Archangel

✪ Moscow

Norwegian Sea

Gulf of Bothnia

Baltic Sea

Sea of Azov

Black Sea

Aegean Sea

Athens ✪

North Sea

London ✪

Celtic Sea

Bay of Biscay

Madrid ✪

Adriatic Sea

Ionian Sea

Palermo •

M e d i t e r r a n e a n S e a

NORTH ATLANTIC OCEAN

Key
Temperature °C

	Over 10
	5–10
	0–5
	0–-5
	-5–-10
	Below -10

✪ Capital city

• Other city or town

One millimetre on this map is the same as 45 kilometres on the ground.

0 10 20 30

EUROPE in summer

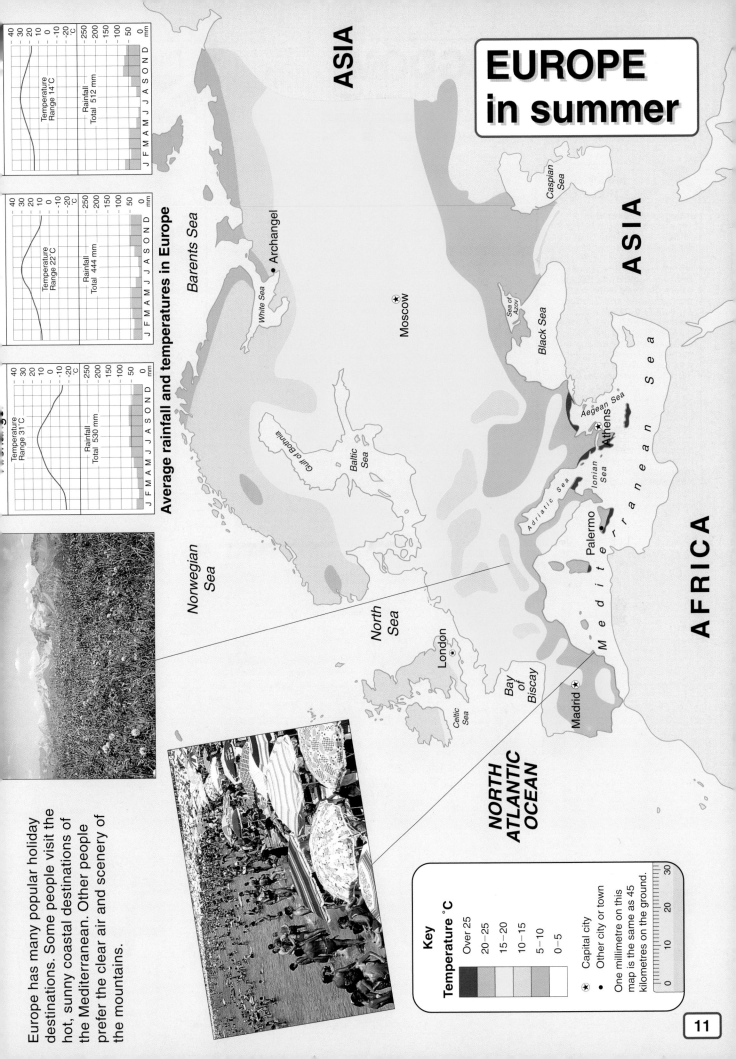

Average rainfall and temperatures in Europe

Europe has many popular holiday destinations. Some people visit the hot, sunny coastal destinations of the Mediterranean. Other people prefer the clear air and scenery of the mountains.

Climate graphs

Temperature Range 14°C — Rainfall Total 512 mm
J F M A M J J A S O N D
40 30 20 10 0 -10 -20 °C
250 200 150 100 50 0 mm

Temperature Range 22°C — Rainfall Total 444 mm
J F M A M J J A S O N D
40 30 20 10 0 -10 -20 °C
250 200 150 100 50 0 mm

Temperature Range 31°C — Rainfall Total 530 mm
J F M A M J J A S O N D
40 30 20 10 0 -10 -20 °C
250 200 150 100 50 0 mm

Map labels

ASIA
AFRICA

NORTH ATLANTIC OCEAN
Norwegian Sea
North Sea
Barents Sea
White Sea
Celtic Sea
Bay of Biscay
Baltic Sea
Gulf of Bothnia
Black Sea
Sea of Azov
Caspian Sea
Aegean Sea
Ionian Sea
Adriatic Sea
Mediterranean Sea

Archangel
Moscow
London
Madrid
Palermo
Athens

Key

Temperature °C
Over 25
20 – 25
15 – 20
10 – 15
5 – 10
0 – 5

★ Capital city
• Other city or town

One millimetre on this map is the same as 45 kilometres on the ground.

0 10 20 30

UNITED KINGDOM Political

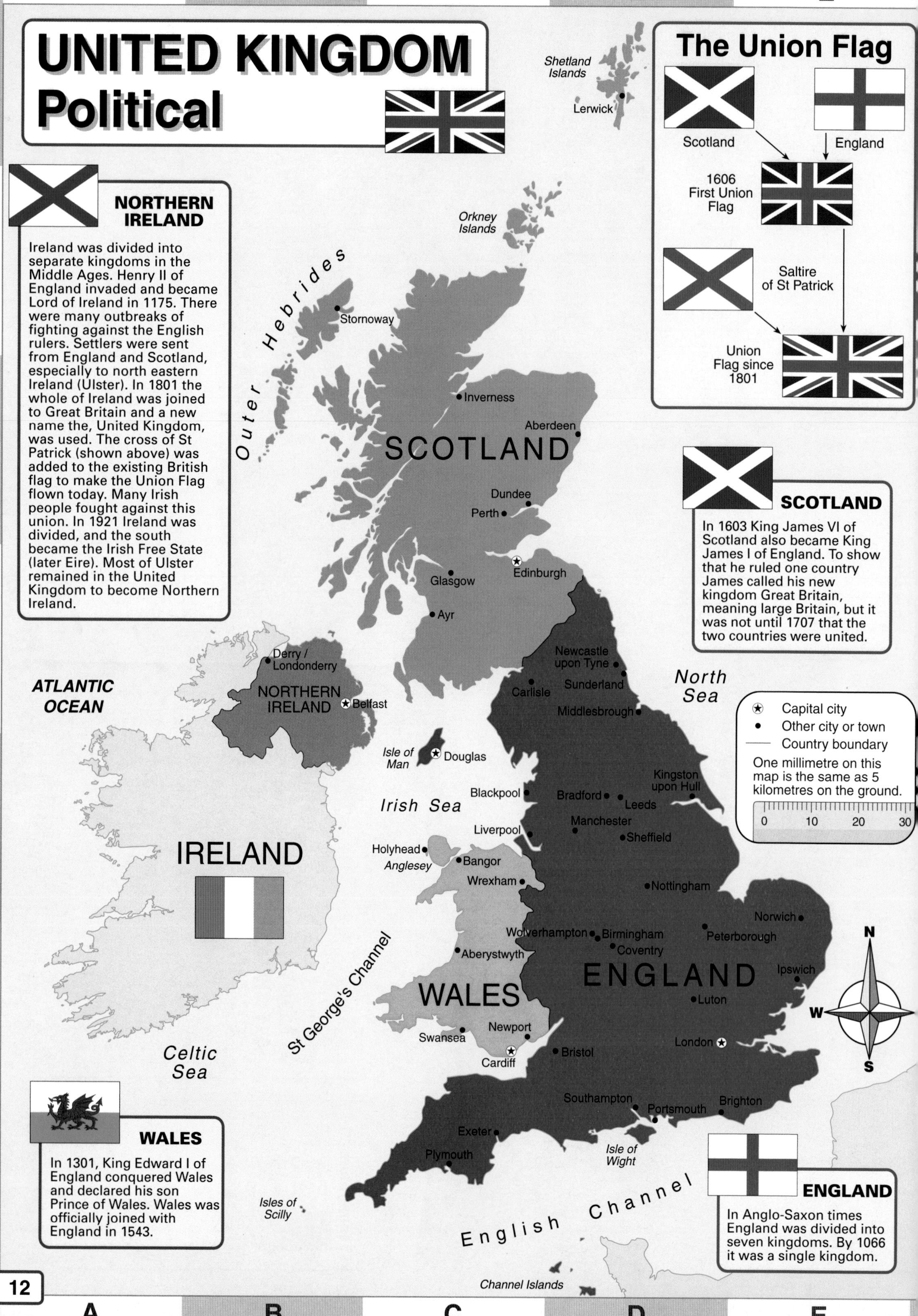

The Union Flag

Scotland
England
1606 First Union Flag
Saltire of St Patrick
Union Flag since 1801

Shetland Islands
Lerwick

NORTHERN IRELAND

Ireland was divided into separate kingdoms in the Middle Ages. Henry II of England invaded and became Lord of Ireland in 1175. There were many outbreaks of fighting against the English rulers. Settlers were sent from England and Scotland, especially to north eastern Ireland (Ulster). In 1801 the whole of Ireland was joined to Great Britain and a new name the, United Kingdom, was used. The cross of St Patrick (shown above) was added to the existing British flag to make the Union Flag flown today. Many Irish people fought against this union. In 1921 Ireland was divided, and the south became the Irish Free State (later Eire). Most of Ulster remained in the United Kingdom to become Northern Ireland.

Orkney Islands

Outer Hebrides

Stornoway

Inverness

Aberdeen

SCOTLAND

In 1603 King James VI of Scotland also became King James I of England. To show that he ruled one country James called his new kingdom Great Britain, meaning large Britain, but it was not until 1707 that the two countries were united.

Dundee
Perth
Glasgow
Edinburgh
Ayr

Derry / Londonderry

NORTHERN IRELAND

Belfast

ATLANTIC OCEAN

Newcastle upon Tyne
Sunderland
Carlisle
Middlesbrough

North Sea

★ Capital city
● Other city or town
— Country boundary

One millimetre on this map is the same as 5 kilometres on the ground.

0   10   20   30

Isle of Man
Douglas

Blackpool
Bradford
Kingston upon Hull
Leeds

Irish Sea

Liverpool
Manchester
Sheffield

Holyhead
Anglesey
Bangor

IRELAND

Wrexham

Nottingham

Norwich

Wolverhampton Birmingham
Coventry
Peterborough

Aberystwyth

ENGLAND

Ipswich

WALES

Luton

London

St George's Channel

Newport
Swansea
Cardiff

Bristol

Celtic Sea

Southampton
Portsmouth
Brighton

N
W   E
S

WALES

In 1301, King Edward I of England conquered Wales and declared his son Prince of Wales. Wales was officially joined with England in 1543.

Exeter
Plymouth

Isle of Wight

ENGLAND

In Anglo-Saxon times England was divided into seven kingdoms. By 1066 it was a single kingdom.

Isles of Scilly

English Channel

Channel Islands

This satellite image is not what you could actually see from space. The satellite has taken many photos of the United Kingdom and a computer has turned these into a single image we can understand. The Earth is curved, so the computer adjusts the images to produce a flat picture. This image helps show population density.

UNITED KINGDOM
Population

The density of population is the number of people living in one square kilometre of land. Different parts of the UK have different population densities.

In northern Scotland there are fewer than 25 people for every square kilometre. In parts of London 10 000 people live in a square kilometre.

Key

Pasture

Arable Land

Urban Areas

Coastal Sand

Mixed Moorland & Forest

One millimetre on this map is the same as 5 kilometres on the ground.

0   10   20   30

More than nine out of ten people live in towns and cities in the UK. This is one of the highest figures in the world.

Fewer than two people out of 100 work in farming in the UK. This is one of the lowest figures in the world.

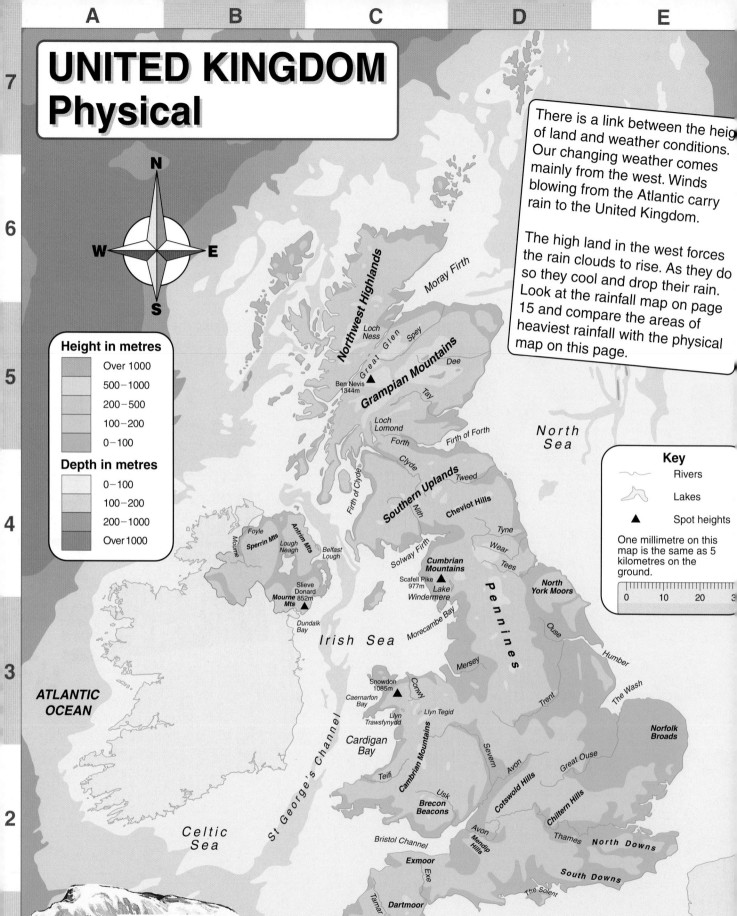

UNITED KINGDOM
Physical

There is a link between the heig of land and weather conditions. Our changing weather comes mainly from the west. Winds blowing from the Atlantic carry rain to the United Kingdom.

The high land in the west forces the rain clouds to rise. As they do so they cool and drop their rain. Look at the rainfall map on page 15 and compare the areas of heaviest rainfall with the physical map on this page.

Height in metres
- Over 1000
- 500 – 1000
- 200 – 500
- 100 – 200
- 0 – 100

Depth in metres
- 0 – 100
- 100 – 200
- 200 – 1000
- Over 1000

Key
- Rivers
- Lakes
- ▲ Spot heights

One millimetre on this map is the same as 5 kilometres on the ground.

0   10   20   3

N
W   E
S

Northwest Highlands
Moray Firth
Loch Ness
Great Glen
Spey
Grampian Mountains
Dee
Ben Nevis 1344m ▲
Tay
Loch Lomond
Forth
Firth of Forth
North Sea
Clyde
Southern Uplands
Nith
Tweed
Cheviot Hills
Firth of Clyde
Tyne
Wear
Solway Firth
Tees
Cumbrian Mountains
Scafell Pike 977m ▲
Lake Windermere
North York Moors
Pennines
Foyle
Antrim Mts
Sperrin Mts
Lough Neagh
Belfast Lough
Mourne
Slieve Donard 852m ▲
Mourne Mts
Dundalk Bay
Morecambe Bay
Irish Sea
Mersey
Ouse
Humber
The Wash
Snowdon 1085m ▲
Conwy
Trent
Caernarfon Bay
Llyn Tegid
Norfolk Broads
Llyn Trawsfynydd
Cardigan Bay
Cambrian Mountains
Severn
Avon
Great Ouse
Cotswold Hills
Chiltern Hills
Teifi
St George's Channel
Usk
Brecon Beacons
Avon
Thames
North Downs
Mendip Hills
ATLANTIC OCEAN
Celtic Sea
Bristol Channel
Exmoor
Exe
South Downs
The Solent
Tamar
Dartmoor
Land's End
English Channel

Ben Nevis 1344m
Snowdon 1085m
Scafell Pike 977m
Slieve Donard 852m

Highest mountains in each country

The satellite image on page 13 shows that most large cities are on low land, away from high mountains.

elief rainfall

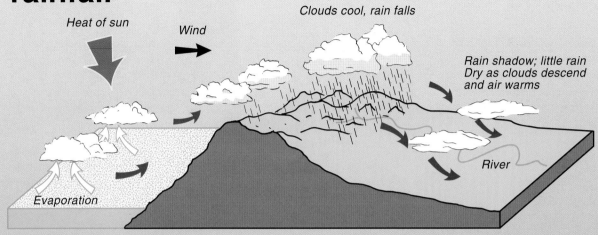

Heat of sun

Wind

Clouds cool, rain falls

Rain shadow; little rain
Dry as clouds descend
and air warms

River

Evaporation

is rainfall map shows that most
n falls on the mountains,
pecially in the far west where
v people live.

Rainfall is low in the South East and eastern England. Droughts are common. This is made worse as the need for water is growing as people move to the area to find work.

Rainfall (mm)

- More than 1800
- 1200 – 1800
- 800 – 1200
- 600 – 800
- 0 – 600

In 1894 Manchester City Corporation had a 96 mile (154 km) aqueduct built from Thirlmere, a lake in the Lake District, to Manchester to provide water for the people and for industry.

GEOLOGY

Geology is the study of the Earth beneath our feet. This map shows the main types of rock found in the United Kingdom.

The rock type can influence industry. Many homes in Britain have slate roofs made from the finest Welsh slate.

In parts of eastern England the sea easily erodes the clay cliffs. Cliff-top houses are destroyed each year.

Different rock types provide suitable locations for differer plants. For example, Bloody Cranesbill grows on limesto wild thyme thrives on chalk.

One millimetre on this map is the same as 6 kilometres on the ground.

0   10   20   30

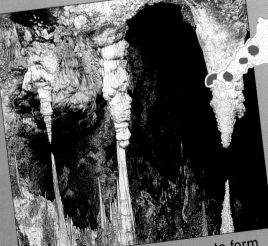

Water can dissolve limestone to form underground caves.

Key

Sedimentary:		Formed from tiny water creatures, plants, sand and mud that sa to the bed of rivers or the sea and were squeezed togeth Limestone, chalk, sandstone and mudstone are all sedimenta
Chalk		A white fine-grained limestone made of tiny sea creatur
Limestone		Carboniferous limestone is hard and grey. It is made of shelled s creatures.
Igneous:		Deep below the Earth's surface are rocks so hot that they are liqu (magma).
Volcanic		Igneous rock which has cooled at or near the Earth's surfa (for example, basalt).
Intrusive		Igneous rock which cooled more slowly below the Earth's surfa (for example, granite).
Metamorphic:		Rocks that have changed by being heated or squeezed (for example, slate and marble).

RIVERS AND LAKES

ers were once main routes for travelling oss the country. The Vikings sailed their ps up the rivers to raid and later to settle. ndon was once the world's busiest port. ps sailed up the Thames to the many ndon docks.

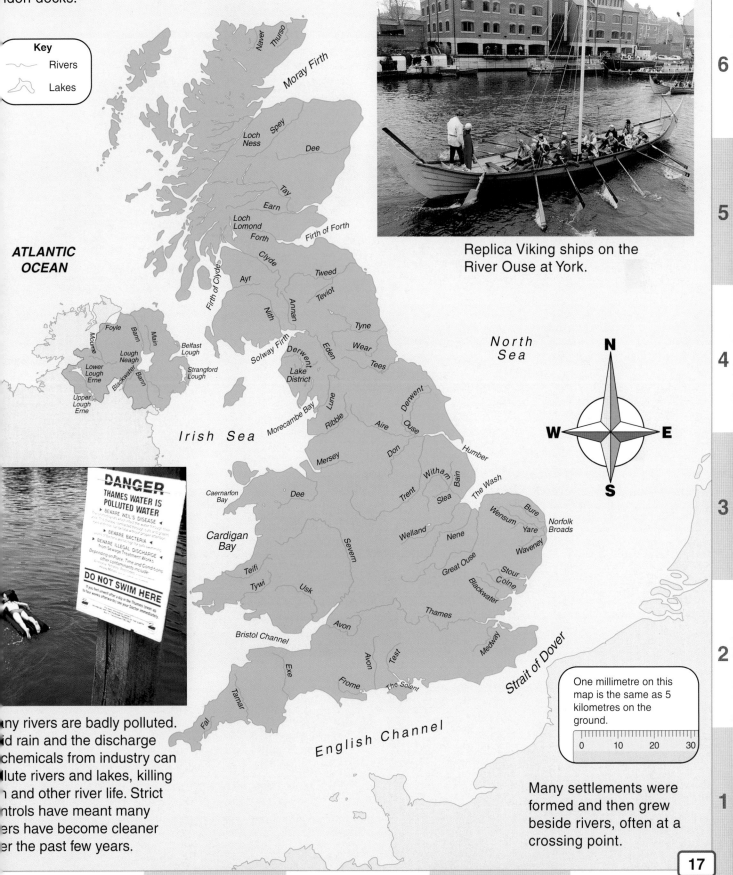

Replica Viking ships on the River Ouse at York.

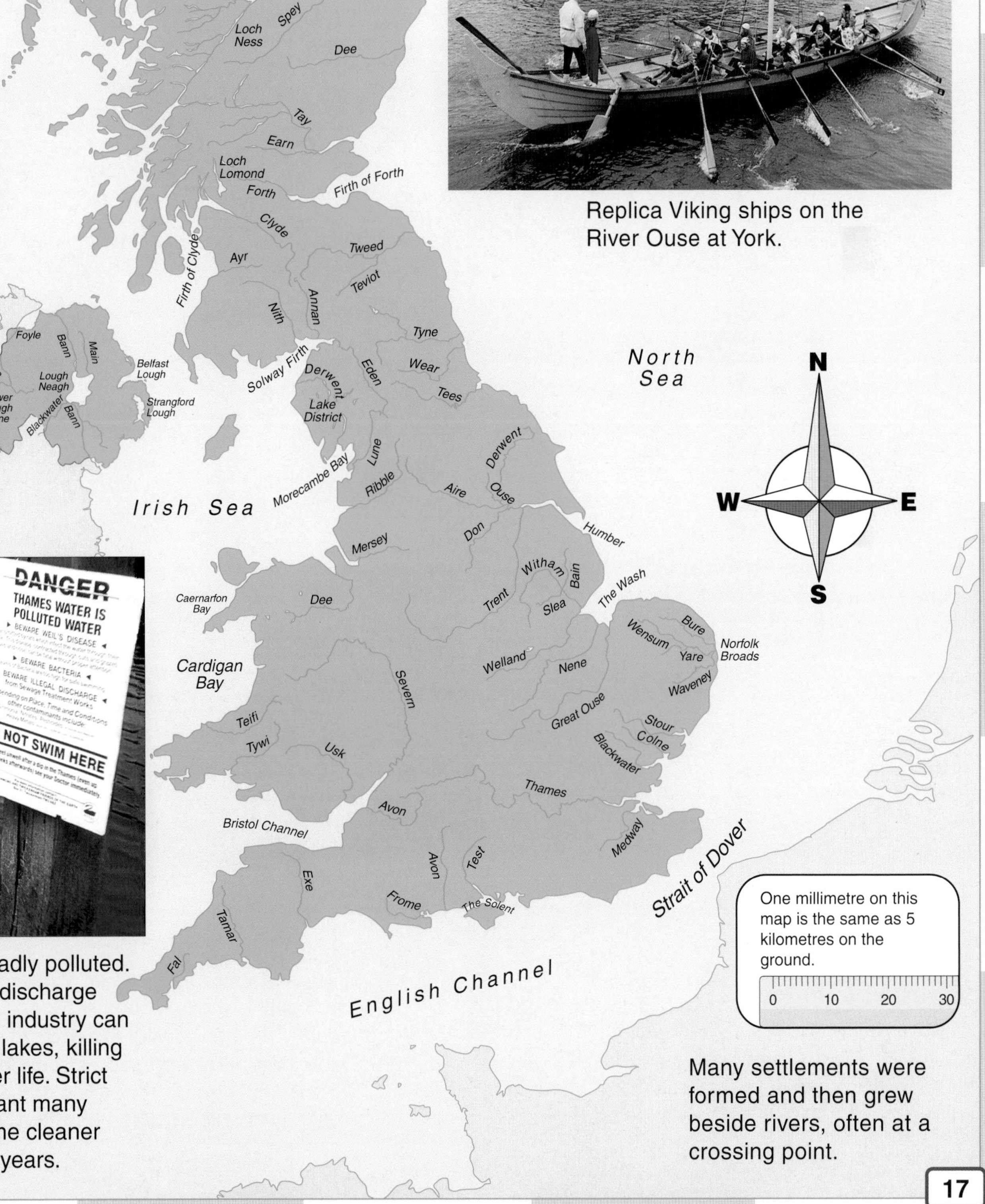

Key
Rivers
Lakes
ATLANTIC OCEAN
Naver
Thurso
Moray Firth
Spey
Loch Ness
Dee
Tay
Earn
Loch Lomond
Forth
Firth of Forth
Clyde
Firth of Clyde
Ayr
Tweed
Teviot
Nith
Annan
Tyne
Foyle
Bann
Main
Mourne
Lough Neagh
Belfast Lough
Lower Lough Erne
Blackwater
Bann
Strangford Lough
Upper Lough Erne
Solway Firth
Derwent
Eden
Wear
Tees
Lake District
North Sea
Lune
Derwent
Morecambe Bay
Ribble
Aire
Ouse
Irish Sea
Mersey
Don
Humber
Witham
Bain
Caernarfon Bay
Dee
Trent
Slea
The Wash
Bure
Wensum
Yare
Norfolk Broads
Cardigan Bay
Severn
Welland
Nene
Waveney
Teifi
Great Ouse
Stour
Colne
Tywi
Usk
Blackwater
Thames
Avon
Bristol Channel
Medway
Exe
Avon
Test
Strait of Dover
Frome
The Solent
Tamar
Fal
English Channel
N
W
E
S
One millimetre on this map is the same as 5 kilometres on the ground.
0
10
20
30

DANGER
THAMES WATER IS POLLUTED WATER
BEWARE WEIL'S DISEASE
BEWARE BACTERIA
BEWARE ILLEGAL DISCHARGE
DO NOT SWIM HERE

ıny rivers are badly polluted. id rain and the discharge chemicals from industry can llute rivers and lakes, killing ı and other river life. Strict ntrols have meant many ers have become cleaner er the past few years.

Many settlements were formed and then grew beside rivers, often at a crossing point.

7
6
5
4
3
2
1

WINTER WEATHER in the UK

In winter the west of Britain is warmer than inland and the east. The sea has a warming effect on the land, raising temperatures near the coast. Towns are warmer than country areas.

Temperature (°C)
Average January temperature

More than 7°
6–7°
5–6°
4–5°
3–4°
Less than 3°

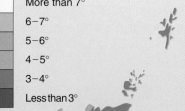

More snow falls on higher ground than on lower ground. There is more snow in the north than the south. Snow forms in clouds which are at freezing temperatures and below.

Snow laying
Average number of mornings with lying snow

0–10
11–20
21–50
Over 50

Fog is tiny droplets of water in the air. On a night without cloud the earth loses heat rapidly. The air above the ground also cools. Moisture in the air turns to droplets, especially twhere there is pollution. When there is no wind the fog can last all day.

e south of Britain is much warmer than the rth. The coast is cooler than inland because e sea has a cooling effect on the land.

st lightning occurs in summer. An electric arge builds up in a cloud and this is scharged to another cloud or to the ground. is lightning spark heats the air causing an plosion, which we hear as thunder. Eastern gland has the most thunderstorms.

Temperature (°C)
Average July temperatures.

	More than 17°
	16°–17°
	15°–16°
	14°–15°
	13°–14°
	Less than 13°

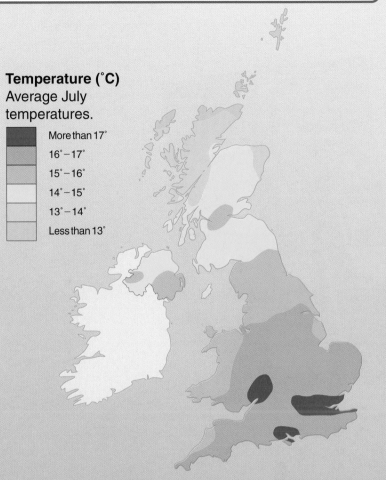

unshine
erage daily duration bright sunshine, hours.

	More than 5.0
	4.5–5.0
	4.0–4.5
	3.5–4.0
	3.0–3.5
	Less than 3.0

The long daylight hours of summer mean most sunshine occurs in June. The least sunshine is in December. The cloudier and wetter areas have least sunshine.

Cumulus clouds form when the sun heats the ground. The air above the ground warms and rises. As it rises it cools and water vapour changes to tiny droplets. Power stations can also produce cumulus clouds.

19

COMMUNICATIONS

More and more people own cars and use them for travel to work. Many motorways in the United Kingdom are jammed with traffic, made worse by road repairs.

One solution is to increase the number of people using public transport. However, that means more fast, reliable buses and trains at a price that people can afford.

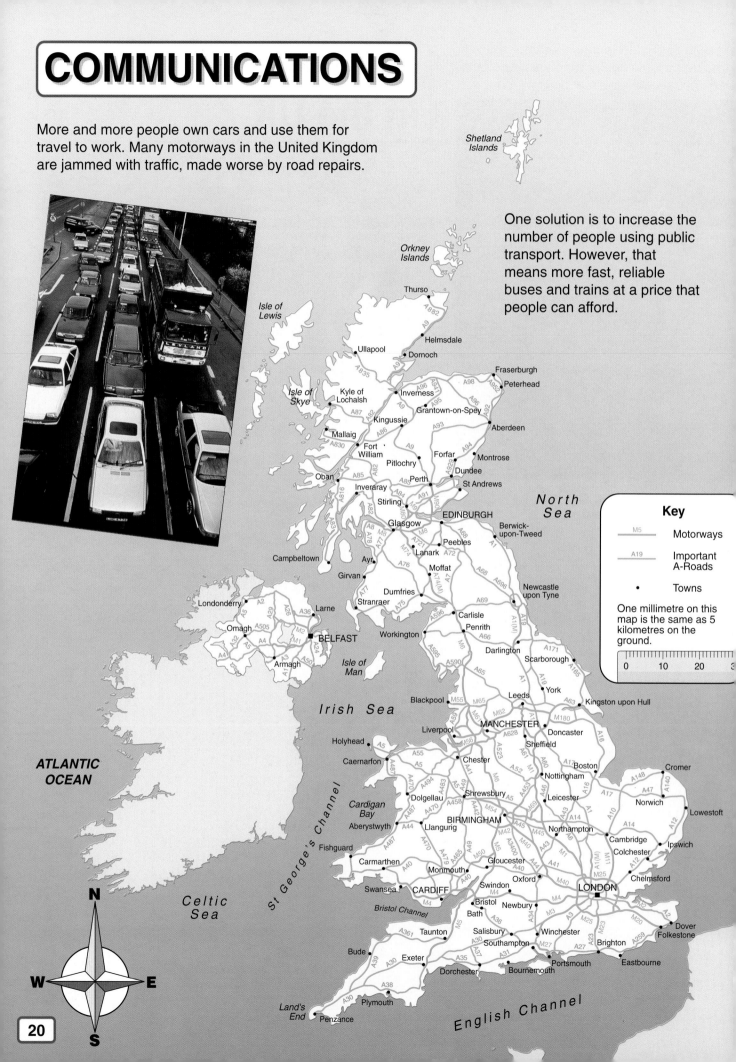

Key

M5	Motorways
A19	Important A-Roads
•	Towns

One millimetre on this map is the same as 5 kilometres on the ground.

0   10   20   3

The development of the railways

The world's first steam railways were in the United Kingdom. The Stockton–Darlington railway opened in 1825. The first intercity railway joined Manchester to Liverpool in 1830.

1851

By 1851 most large towns were linked by railways.

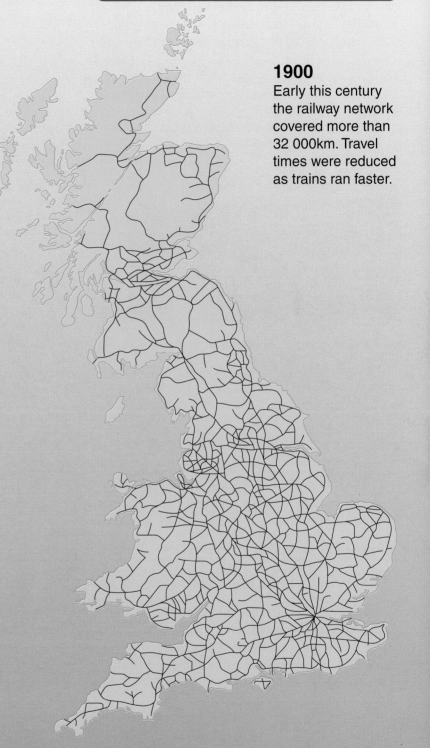

1900

Early this century the railway network covered more than 32 000km. Travel times were reduced as trains ran faster.

1995

In the 1930s road building began to increase. Other forms of transport began to replace the train. In the 1960s many railway lines and small stations were closed.

TRANSPORT

The Romans constructed roads throughout Britain, so that the army could be moved quickly wherever it was needed and trade could develop. London, the main city and port, was linked to all parts by major roads.

Many of these roads were kept in good repair even after the Romans left Britain in AD409.

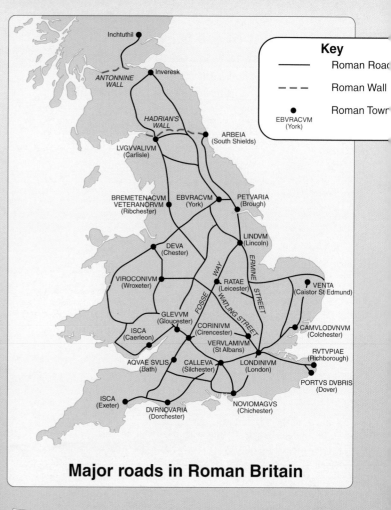

Major roads in Roman Britain

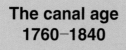

The canal age 1760–1840

Road communications were poor for many centuries. In the eighteenth century much of Britain's trade travelled by sea around the coast rather than across country.

In the 1760s canal building began. Cities were linked for trade and transport was better and cheaper. The railways (see page 21) took much of the canal trade in the next century. Today the canal and river system of Great Britain covers 3,200 km of water. Three-quarters of it is used for leisure boating and fishing.

In 1958 the first stretch of motorway in Britain was opened. It was called the Preston bypass and is now part of the M6. In 1959 a large part of the M1 was opened. Unlike earlier main roads, motorways are designed to avoid town centres and reduce journey times.

Motorways in 1964

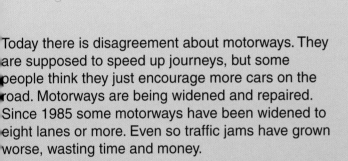

Today there is disagreement about motorways. They are supposed to speed up journeys, but some people think they just encourage more cars on the road. Motorways are being widened and repaired. Since 1985 some motorways have been widened to eight lanes or more. Even so traffic jams have grown worse, wasting time and money.

Today's motorways

SCOTLAND

The north and west of Scotland has high mountains, magnificent scenery, high rainfall and few people. Most of the population lives in lowland Scotland. Oil and gas discoveries in the North Sea have brought jobs and money to the north-east of Scotland. The Foinavon Field is a new oilfield in the North Atlantic Ocean where the sea is much deeper.

People all over the world have heard of the Loch Ness Monster. Loch Ness is one of the lochs in the Great Glen, a deep valley which divides the Scottish Highlands.

In the Past

The Romans built Hadrian's Wall to keep the Picts and Scots out. Angles and Vikings later settled in Scotland. The country was united in the ninth century under King Kenneth I. In 1296 Edward I of England claimed the Scottish throne but Robert the Bruce forced the English out. In 1603 King James VI of Scotland became King James I of England.

Largest Settlements

Glasgow	697 000
Edinburgh	438 000
Aberdeen	211 000
Dundee	175 000
Paisley	95 000

■ 100 000 people

Scotland has the finest winter sports in the United Kingdom. Aviemore is the best known centre.

Shetland's Viking past is still celebrated today.

CENTRAL SCOTLAND

M4 ◈	Motorway, service area
	Motorway, junction
A31	Primary route
A475	Other main road
	Passenger railway
	County boundary
	National boundary
✈ ✈	Airport / with Customs
⛴	International ferry port
⛴	Domestic ferry port
	City / Urban area
○	Town area
	River / Lake

	800m +
	600 - 800m
	400 - 600m
	200 - 400m
	75 - 200m
	0 - 75m

One millimetre on the map is the same as 1 kilometre on the ground

0   10   20   30   40

Most of Scotland's population lives in the lowland central area. The two great cities of Glasgow and Edinburgh are located here.

In 1750 Edinburgh was the second largest city in the British Isles. In the early nineteenth century Glasgow became Scotland's largest city. Glasgow's population grew to over one million in the 1950s.

Central Scotland was once a great engineering centre. Ships, railway engines and machinery were built and exported around the world. These industries have shrunk leading to large scale unemployment.

Edinburgh has always been a popular city for tourists. Its famous castle and arts festival attract visitors from all over the world.

Tourism and office jobs have increased in Glasgow, where modern offices have appeared next to the city's historic buildings.

New industry has been attracted to central Scotland. High technology linked to computers has produced new jobs in electronics.

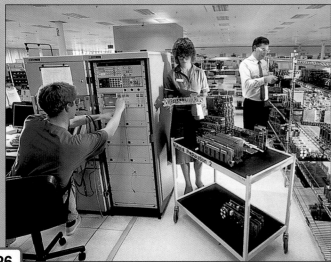

WALES

Wales is a country of great contrasts. South Wales is very densely populated, especially in the valleys which lead down to Cardiff. In parts of central and North Wales the sheep outnumber the people. The Welsh mountains contain many rare plants. Tourists, especially climbers and walkers, are attracted to the rugged beauty of the land.

Key

M4	Motorway, service area
	Motorway, junction
A31	Primary route
A475	Other main road
	Passenger railway
	County boundary
	National boundary
✈ ✈	Airport / with Customs
	International ferry port
	Domestic ferry port
	City / Urban area
○	Town area
	River / Lake

	800m +
	600 - 800m
	400 - 600m
	200 - 400m
	75 - 200m
	0 - 75m

One millimetre on the map is the same as 1 kilometre on the ground

```
0    10    20    30    40
```

In the Past

Different rulers of England tried to conquer Wales but always found the mountains a great problem. There the Welsh could avoid invaders and attack them when ready. In the Middle Ages the English kings built magnificent castles and towns into which they moved settlers in an attempt to control the Welsh.

The Welsh language is strongest in North Wales but is growing in popularity in other parts of Wales. About 20% of people speak Welsh.

Dim palmant am 800 llath
No footway for 800yds

Largest Settlements

Swansea	282 000
Cardiff	279 000
Newport	104 000
Ebbw Vale	77 000
Merthyr Tydfil	57 000

100 000 people

Wales has been very successful in attracting Japanese companies to build factories. These have helped replace the jobs lost by the decline of industries such as coal, steel and slate.

NORTH WEST ENGLAND

North West England is a very varied region. The Pennines contain many towns which grew rapidly during the nineteenth century, their industry based on textiles. The Lake District is possibly England's most beautiful area. The south contains great cities like Manchester and Liverpool, famous for their industry, music and football.

Blackpool Pleasure Beach is the United Kingdom's most popular tourist attraction and Blackpool is the busiest seaside holiday resort. Rides like 'The Big One' attract millions of visitors.

Largest Settlements

Settlement	Population
Manchester	450 000
Liverpool	450 000
Salford	350 000
Stockport	292 000
Warrington	190 000

100 000 people

In the Past

The Romans built major towns like Chester and Manchester as well as forts all the way to Hadrian's Wall. Later most of the region became Saxon but Norwegian Vikings settled in the Lake District and near the coast. Large numbers of people from all over the British Isles and Europe set out for new lives in America from the port of Liverpool.

The Lake District has magnificent mountains, lakes and valleys. It is England's wettest area but remains very popular with visitors. It was home to many great poets.

NORTH EAST ENGLAND

York was an important city in Roman times and in the Viking period. The name York comes from the Danish name Jorvik. Today, York is an important tourist city, attracting people from all around the world.

Older industries were based on coal and iron which were mined in the region. Wool, from sheep in the hills, was turned into cloth in the towns east of the Pennines. In 1913 30% of the world's ships were built in the region, but today the industry has almost disappeared.

Key

M4 ⓢ	Motorway, service area
	Motorway, junction
A31	Primary route
A475	Other main road
	Passenger railway
	County boundary
	National boundary
✈ ⊕	Airport / with Customs
⛴	International ferry port
⛴	Domestic ferry port
	City / Urban area
○	Town area
	River / Lake

	800m +
	600 - 800m
	400 - 600m
	200 - 400m
	75 - 200m
	0 - 75m

One millimetre on the map is the same as 1 kilometre on the ground

```
0    10    20    30    40
```

Largest Settlements

Leeds	450 000
Bradford	295 000
Kingston upon Hull	245 000
Newcastle	200 000
Sunderland	190 000

100 000 people

In the Past

The Romans built Hadrian's Wall which reached the North Sea near Newcastle upon Tyne. In Anglo-Saxon times the region was part of the Kingdom of Northumbria. Viking raiders found it easy to sail to this coast and Danish Vikings settled in large numbers. In the Middle Ages more abbeys and monasteries were built here than in any other region of Britain.

Most new jobs are in services. The Metro Centre near Gateshead attracts shoppers from long distances.

In Leeds, office jobs have increased. The first 'telephone bank' in Britain is based there.

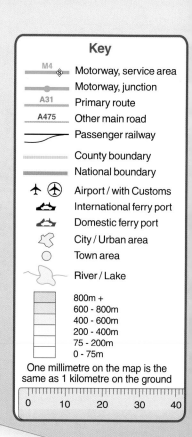

A   **B**   **C**   **D**   **E**   **F**

1° 30' W   1° 00' W   0° 30' W   0° 00'   0° 30' E   1° 00' E

erwick-upon-Tweed

Holy Island

5

poler

55° 30' N

Alnwick

N

Amble

NORTHUMBERLAND

4

W   E

Morpeth

Bedlington

Ashington

S

Blyth

ewcastle
pon Tyne   **Tynemouth**

55° 00' N

rbridge

South Shields

TYNE & WEAR

Gateshead

onsett   **Sunderland**

Chester-
le-Street   Seaham

3

DURHAM   **Durham**

Peterlee

Bishop
Auckland   Crook

Hartlepool

CLEVELAND

arnard
Castle   Newton
Aycliffe   **Stockton-
on-Tees**

Redcar

Darlington

Middlesbrough

Guisborough

cotch Corner

Teeside
Airport

Whitby

R Esk

Richmond

Leyburn   Northallerton

2

**NORTH
YORKSHIRE**

Thirsk

Pickering

Scarborough

Filey

Ripon

Easingwold

Malton

Flamborough Head

Knaresborough

Bridlington

54° 00' N

*Bridlington
Bay*

skipton   **Harrogate**

Driffield

HUMBERSIDE

York

Ilkley   Wetherby

Hornsea

Keighley

Leeds   Tadcaster

Market
Weighton

Beverley

1

Bradford   Selby

**Kingston
upon Hull**

lifax   Dewsbury

Castleford

Howden

Humber
Bridge

Withernsea

R Humber

M62

Wakefield   Pontefract

Goole

*Spurn
Head*

Huddersfield   **Barnsley**

Thorne

Scunthorpe

Immingham

Holmfirth   **SOUTH YORKSHIRE**

Brigg

Grimsby

on-under-Lyne
Glossop

Doncaster

Humberside
Airport

53° 30' N

NORTH SEA

54° 30' N

0° 30' W   0° 00'   0° 30' E

A   **B**   **C**   **D**   **E**   **F**

MIDLANDS

Birmingham is the United Kingdom's second largest city. During the Industrial Revolution, Birmingham expanded rapidly. Unusually for a large city, it is not built on a river but it does have a network of canals.

Key

M4 ⓢ	Motorway, service area
	Motorway, junction
A31	Primary route
A475	Other main road
	Passenger railway
	County boundary
	National boundary
✈ ✈	Airport / with Customs
	International ferry port
	Domestic ferry port
	City / Urban area
○	Town area
	River / Lake

800m +
600 - 800m
400 - 600m
200 - 400m
75 - 200m
0 - 75m

One millimetre on the map is the same as 1 kilometre on the ground

0   10   20   30   40

Largest Settlements

Birmingham	1 000 000
Sheffield	528 000
Coventry	300 000
Leicester	280 000
Nottingham	280 000

■ 1 million people
■ 100 000 people

In the Past

The Romans conquered the region and it became Romanised. Anglo-Saxons settled there after the Roman withdrawal. The region was part of the Kingdom of Mercia. King Offa of Mercia had a great ditch dug to mark the boundary between Mercia and Wales. It can still be walked along today. Later the region was attacked by Vikings and also by Welsh raiders who came from their hills, stole animals and goods, and returned. The world's first iron bridge was built at Ironbridge in 1778 – it crosses the River Severn.

The car industry has been based in the region for many years. Rolls Royce, Jaguar and Land Rover, three of the world's best-known car names, are all based there.

The National Exhibition Centre (NEC) has been built at Birmingham, attracting international visitors to major events.

EAST MIDLANDS and EAST ANGLIA

Key

M4 ⓢ	Motorway, service area
	Motorway, junction
A31	Primary route
A475	Other main road
	Passenger railway
	County boundary
	National boundary
✈ ✈	Airport / with Customs
⛴	International ferry port
⛴	Domestic ferry port
	City / Urban area
◯	Town area
	River / Lake

800m +
600 - 800m
400 - 600m
200 - 400m
75 - 200m
0 - 75m

One millimetre on the map is the same as 1 kilometre on the ground

0   10   20   30   40

The region is the flattest in the United Kingdom. Some of the land east of Peterborough is below sea level. It was marshland until the land was drained – now it is rich farm land. The town of Ely stands on high ground which was once an island.

In the west of the region are large cities and coalfields. Close to Nottingham is the remains of Sherwood Forest – the setting for the legendary adventures of Robin Hood and his merry men.

This helmet was part of the remains found in the burial ship at Sutton Hoo. King Radwald died in about AD625 and was buried in his ship beneath a huge mound of soil.

In the Past

The Roman occupation of Britain was seriously threatened when Queen Boudicca led her tribe, the Iceni, against the Romans. The Roman colony at Colchester was destroyed before Boudicca was defeated. Following the departure of the Romans the region was conquered first by Anglo-Saxons and later by Danish Vikings.

Largest Settlements

Northampton	186 000	
Norwich	173 000	
Colchester	151 000	
Peterborough	136 000	
Ipswich	120 000	

100 000 people

East of Norwich are the Norfolk Broads – an area of lakes, rivers and channels. Tourists come here for boating holidays. It is also home to many rare birds, flowers, insects and plants.

Some of the world's best racehorses are trained in the Newmarket area.

SOUTH EAST and CENTRAL SOUTHERN ENGLAND

London is the hub of this region. Motorways, roads and railways run out from London, like the spokes of a wheel, to the rest of the region. Every week millions of people travel into London to work, shop or visit.

London was once the world's largest city. Today it is an important world centre for trade, industry, banking, entertainment and tourism. Parts of old London such as the docklands have been demolished and replaced with modern office blocks and housing.

Key

M4 ⓢ	Motorway, service area
	Motorway, junction
A31	Primary route
A475	Other main road
	Passenger railway
	County boundary
	National boundary
✈ ✈	Airport / with Customs
⛴	International ferry port
⛴	Domestic ferry port
	City / Urban area
○	Town area
	River / Lake

	800m +
	600 - 800m
	400 - 600m
	200 - 400m
	75 - 200m
	0 - 75m

One millimetre on the map is the same as 1 kilometre on the ground

0   10   20   30   40

Largest Settlements

London	7 650 000
Southampton	196 000
Milton Keynes	184 000
Portsmouth	181 000
Swindon	173 000

1 million people
100 000 people

The airports of the South East include Heathrow, the world's busiest airport for international passengers.

In the Past

Invaders and settlers have entered the region from Continental Europe throughout history. Julius Caesar came briefly in 55BC, but a full Roman invasion had to wait until AD43. The Romans soon took control of the South East. They founded London, which became the capital of Roman Britain. In the fifth century, the region was invaded by Anglo-Saxons and Jutes. The rule of the Anglo-Saxons lasted until the Vikings conquered the South East. In 1066 William the Conqueror landed at Pevensey, near Hastings. This was the last successful invasion of England.

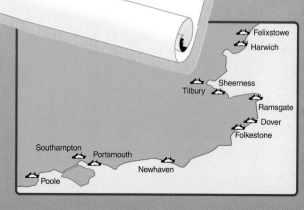

Felixstowe
Harwich
Sheerness
Tilbury
Ramsgate
Dover
Folkestone
Southampton
Portsmouth
Newhaven
Poole

The coast is dotted with ports both large and small. Southampton is important both for trade and cruise ships. The QE2 sails from there.

39

SOUTH WEST ENGLAND

South West England contains the beautiful countryside and villages of the Cotswolds, Salisbury Plain where Stonehenge stands and rich farmland around Gloucester and south of Bristol. The hills of the south give way to rugged, wild moorland further west. Dartmoor and Exmoor are both National Parks. They can be dangerous when the snow or mist set in.

Stonehenge is an immense stone circle built around 1500BC. Its exact purpose is unknown.

Key

M4 ⓢ	Motorway, service area
	Motorway, junction
A31	Primary route
A475	Other main road
	Passenger railway
	County boundary
	National boundary
✈ ⓐ	Airport / with Customs
	International ferry port
	Domestic ferry port
	City / Urban area
○	Town area
	River / Lake

	800m +
	600 - 800m
	400 - 600m
	200 - 400m
	75 - 200m
	0 - 75m

One millimetre on the map is the same as 1 kilometre on the ground

0   10   20   30   40

Largest Settlements

Bristol   370 000
Plymouth   242 000
Bournemouth 154 000
Exeter   103 000
Gloucester   97 000

■ 100 000 people

In the Past

There is much evidence of the settlements of the Ancient Britons, like hill-top villages, standing stones, burial chambers and stone circles. The city of Bath was the Roman town Aquae Sulis. Parts of the Roman baths can still be visited today. Bristol, the largest city in the South West, developed on the rivers Severn and Avon. The city grew rich on trade in wool, wine, tobacco, chocolate and slaves. Cornwall remained different from most of England for many centuries. The Cornish language died out but Cornish place names and saints' names remain.

Bristol is another ancient dock city which has had to redevelop its docklands because of changes in trade and the size of ships.

The Atlantic Ocean brings warm sea and air to the South West. Tourists visit the region for the warm summers, sandy beaches and hills. Parts of the region are so busy in summer that towns have been closed to any more traffic.

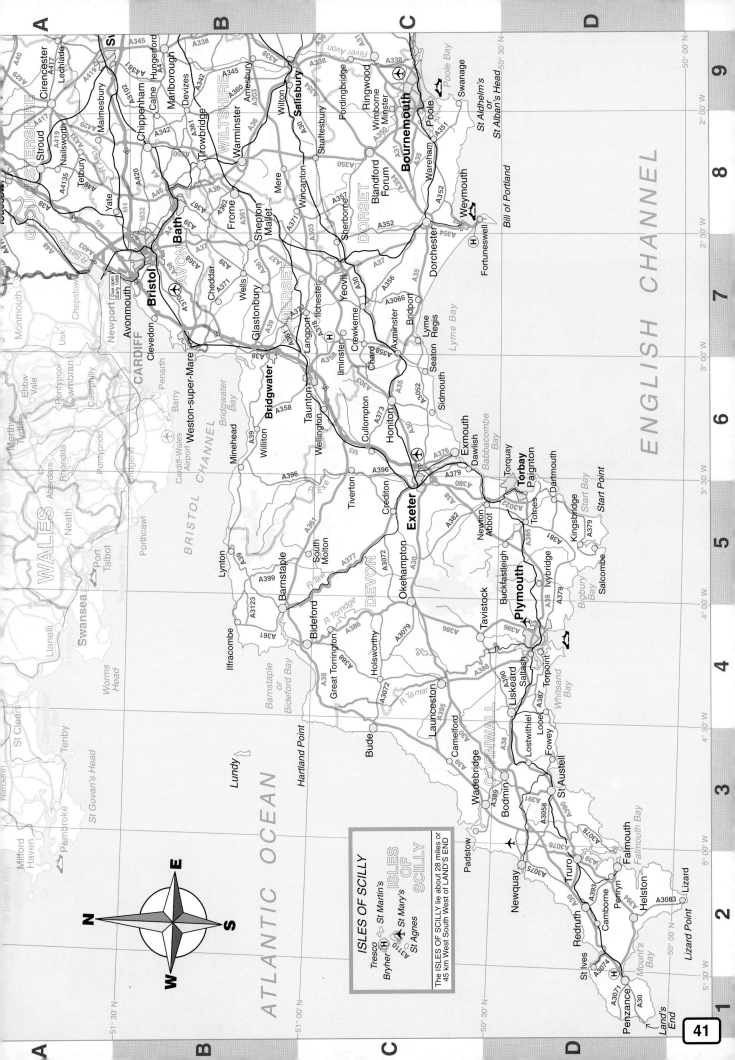

NORTHERN IRELAND

Northern Ireland is a province of just over 1.5 million people. There are only two large settlements in the province, Belfast and Londonderry (Derry). Many people live in small settlements, particularly in the farming areas.

Key

M4 $	Motorway, service area
	Motorway, junction
A31	Primary route
A475	Other main road
	Passenger railway
	County boundary
	National boundary
✈ ✈	Airport / with Customs
	International ferry port
	Domestic ferry port
	City / Urban area
○	Town area
	River / Lake

	800m +
	600 - 800m
	400 - 600m
	200 - 400m
	75 - 200m
	0 - 75m

One millimetre on the map is the same as 1 kilometre on the ground

0   10   20   30   40

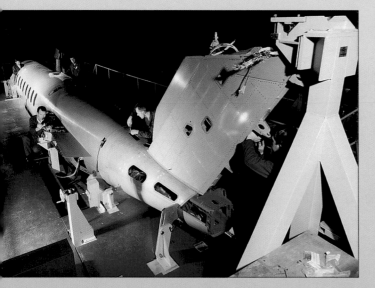

Violence between the Republicans and the Loyalists over many years means industries such as tourism have not developed as strongly as they might. Peace will provide a great economic boost to the area.

Belfast is the largest city in Northern Ireland, although its population has been falling. It was over 400,000 in 1971, but is now about 280,000. Belfast is an industrial city with a port. Shipbuilding and aircraft manufacture are still important industries in the city.

In the Past

What is now Northern Ireland has had several invasions. Both the Vikings and Normans invaded. The English ruled Ireland from the twelfth century, but rebellions were frequent. From the sixteenth century many settlers from England and Scotland moved to Ulster, the north-eastern part of Ireland. In 1921 Ireland was divided. Most of Ulster remained in the UK.

Largest Settlements

Belfast	279 000	▮▮▮
Londonderry/Derry	72 000	▮
Bangor	52 000	▮
Lisburn	42 000	▮
Ballymena	28 000	▮

▮ 100 000 people

Dairy farming is well-suited to the cool, wet climate.

One of Northern Ireland's most famous physical features is the Giant's Causeway. It was formed when volcanic lava broke through the earth's surface. This lava is called basalt. In the open air it began to cool and contracted (shrank) into polygons. From above it looks like a stone honeycomb.